FIGHTER PLANES

BY

BILL GUNSTON OBE FRAeS

The First Fighters

In 1903 the Wright Brothers made the first successful aeroplane flights in the USA. Seven years later, the British Secretary of State for War said, *'We do not consider that aeroplanes will be of any possible use for war purposes.'* This view was held by officials around the world, including in France which rapidly became the centre of aviation pioneering. However, in 1912 the British military formed the Royal Flying Corps (RFC), to fly reconnaissance missions to see what enemy troops were doing. Just for fun, the pilots began firing at kites with rifles and revolvers. By 1913 one of the first military aircraft was put on display by the giant Vickers company. Called the 'Experimental Fighting Biplane', it was specially designed so that a machine gun could be mounted in the nose. When war broke out in Europe in August 1914, Vickers were contracted to produce 50 of their FB.5s and by 1915 over 100 had been sent to France with the RFC squadrons, primarily instructed to ram any Zeppelins encountered on their way. Without parachutes, this was not an exciting prospect for the untrained pilots, who resourcefully wore car tyres in case they came down in the English Channel. Before long two-seater planes were carrying observers with rifles and revolvers trained on the enemy, and combat aircraft became a reality. All this must have been a great shock to the Generals and politicians who had written off aeroplanes as useless in wartime.

ZEPPELIN AIRSHIPS

Before the First World War began in 1914 the idea of aeroplanes in war was remote, but the use of airships was a possibility. Both the German Army and Navy used airships, and from 1915 they used them to drop bombs on Britain. It took aeroplanes to shoot them down.

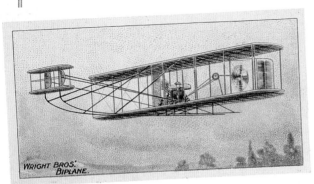

WRIGHT BROS. BIPLANE.

WRIGHT BIPLANE

In August 1910 Lt Jake Fickel, of the US Army, flew as passenger in a Wright biplane and fired four shots from a Springfield rifle at a target almost one metre (3 feet) square on the ground. He scored two hits. He was the first man ever to fire a gun from an aeroplane.

EXPÉRIENCES DE LANCEMENT DE BOMBES EN AÉROPLANE

THE FRENCH AIR CORPS

This illustration depicts early manoeuvres by the rench Air Corps in 1913, showing them dropping bombs from aeroplanes.

VICKERS GUNBUS

In February 1913 what could be called the first British military aircraft was put on display by Vickers at an Aero Show in London. This 'Experimental Fighting Biplane' (EFB) had quite a short central body (a 'nacelle') with the engine at the back driving a pusher propeller. This meant that the tail had to be attached by four thin rods (called booms), which were far enough apart to leave room for the propeller. This rather strange arrangement was adopted so that the company's own Vickers-Maxim machine gun could be mounted in the nose, fed by a long belt of ammunition. It was aimed by a gunner in the front cockpit. Just behind him was the pilot. This 'pusher' arrangement was later used by many types of aircraft, including the FB.5 (Fighting Biplane, type 5), popularly called the Gunbus, which was active in the First World War.

GUNBUS COCKPIT

Pilots soon discovered that they needed instruments to help them fly. The first were a tachometer (showing how fast the engine was turning), an altimeter (showing how high the aeroplane was flying), and an airspeed indicator (showing speed through the air).

THE PILOT'S SIDEARM

After the War began most reconnaissance pilots carried a personal 'sidearm', for possible use to avoid capture after being shot down. This Webley pistol was a favourite for British pilots.

DROPPING BOMBS

The first bombers were often ordinary aircraft fitted with a bomb-dropping mechanism invented and fitted on the spot. An even simpler answer was for the crew to hang the bombs beside the cockpits and drop them by hand.

Dawn of Air Warfare

In 1912 the British Government decided that perhaps aeroplanes might have some military use. They organized a competition, entered by Geoffrey de Havilland with his B.E.1. Although he did not win, he continued to improve his neat biplane which became the Royal Flying Corps' most numerous type in the First World War. It was a B.E. that was to claim the first air combat victory on 25 August 1914, only three weeks after the start of the War. Three B.E.2s chased a German aircraft for miles before the German pilot, realizing he could not get away, landed in a field. Both occupants escaped to a nearby wood. The British pilots ran after them, brandishing pistols, but returned to set fire to the enemy aircraft and then took off again. A month later, Frenchman Sergeant Joseph Frantz suddenly came up behind a German Aviatik. His Voisin plane was armed with a Hotchkiss machine gun. Quickly his observer, Corporal Louis Quénault, aimed at the enemy aircraft and shot it down. This was the first aircraft actually shot down in air warfare, and the dawn of the aeroplane as a weapon of war.

MACHINE GUN

It was the machine gun that transformed aeroplanes into fighters. In the First World War almost all the machine guns fitted to aircraft were originally designed for use by soldiers on the ground. Many French aircraft used this type of Hotchkiss machine gun, mounted on pivots and aimed by the observer. He was usually in a cockpit behind the pilot, but in the Voisin he was in front.

THE 'BLERIOT EXPERIMENTAL' OR B.E.2

Louis Blériot was a Frenchman who made monoplanes, but his name became synonymous with the RFC for aeroplanes with a propeller on the nose. De Havilland's B.E.2 was popular with the RFC. It was very stable in flight, which meant it could fly without the pilot touching the controls. Therefore both pilot and observer could watch the battlefield below and write down anything of interest. This stability made the aircraft difficult to manoeuvre, which was disastrous against the new German planes in the First World War.

NATIONAL MARKINGS c.1915

Once the War began it was soon realized that aircraft had to be painted with a clear indication of their nationality, so ground soldiers did not shoot at their own aircraft. Soon simple national markings were devised.

Great Britain *Russia* *Belgium* *Italy* *Germany*

MONOPLANE FIGHTERS

The British thought monoplanes unsafe, but the French Morane-Saulnier firm made them in large numbers. This Type L monoplane had the wing passing through the fuselage (body), while other Moranes had it fixed above the fuselage on struts.

The Fokker Scourge

Even before the start of the First World War several far-sighted people had come to the conclusion that the best way for an aeroplane to shoot down an enemy would be for it to have a machine gun fixed to fire straight ahead. It would be aimed by manoeuvring the whole aircraft. Thus, the pilot need be the only person on board, and the aircraft could be smaller and more agile than a two-seater. Of course, with the propeller at the front there was a problem. The French pilot, Roland Garros, just fixed strong steel deflectors to the propeller of his Morane L monoplane at the beginning of the War and quickly destroyed four German aircraft. When Garros was himself shot down, the Germans discovered his idea, and asked Anthony Fokker to copy it. Fokker came up with something better – he invented a way to synchronize the gun to the speed of the propeller, so it only fired when there was no propeller blade in front. The result was the Fokker Eindecker. Though it was a low-powered little aircraft, its combination of adequate speed, excellent manoeuvrability and a forward-firing machine gun made it deadly.

GERMANY'S TOP ACES

Here Baron von Richthofen, Germany's top ace, is surrounded by four of his pilots. When flying, they often left their caps behind but kept on their cavalry boots and heavy leather greatcoats in order to try to keep warm. Their counterparts in the RFC wore a strange double-breasted tunic (popularly called a 'maternity jacket'), and increasingly wore specially designed calf-length soft boots lined with thick fur.

FOKKER TRIPLANE

Officially called the Dr.I, the brightly painted triplanes were as feared as the Eindecker had been previously. Allied planes were usually camouflaged, or just painted a dull olive-brown, but the best German fighters were organized into large groups called circuses, in which each pilot could choose to paint his aircraft in an individual scheme of vivid colours to frighten the enemy. This scarlet one is a replica of that used by the greatest of them all, Baron Manfred von Richthofen (the Red Baron). He held Germany's top-score of 80 victories when he was shot down and killed in April 1918.

ANTHONY FOKKER

Anthony Fokker was a Dutchman, but before the First World War he set up his aircraft factory near Berlin. By the end of the War he was famous (British people would say infamous), and he had no difficulty in moving his factory to his native Amsterdam, where he made everything from fighters to airliners.

D.H.2

Captain Geoffrey de Havilland was one of the most famous British aircraft designers. In 1915 he designed the D.H.2, with a single cockpit in the nose fitted with a machine gun. The D.H.2 was a useful single-seater, but it was the later D.H.4, with its 375-horsepower engine, that became the Allies' most important anti-Zeppelin aircraft.

NIEUPORT XI

The French Nieuport company made some of the best single-seat fighters of their day. The Nie. XI was called *Le Bébé* because it was so small. It had only an 80-horsepower engine and weighed little more than 454 kg (1,000 lb). They were outstandingly agile biplanes that could easily catch the Fokkers and beat them in close combat.

Killing Machines

By 1916 air warfare was an accomplished fact. As well as the task of reconnaissance, aircraft had been developed to drop bombs, aim torpedoes at ships and, not least, shoot down other aircraft. Combat aircraft were at first called 'fighting scouts', but they gradually became known as 'fighters' (except in the USA where until the Second World War they were called 'pursuits'). The key to success in air combat was higher flight performance: faster speed, more rapid climb to greater altitudes, and ever-better ability to manoeuvre. These demands could only be met by fitting more powerful engines. Armaments were also important and many were developed during the First World War. Dozens of different small bombs were tried, and showers of darts. A few pilots even tried to snare enemy aircraft with grappling hooks at the end of a long cable! Night fighters also made their first appearance because of a need to find some aerial defence against German Zeppelin airships.

Armed with a crew, machine guns, an electric generator and a searchlight, they were too slow to be effective. Ordinary fighters were better, and in 1919 the best was the Fokker D.VII. Not particularly special, but extraordinarily effective, the Allies demanded the hand-over of every D.VII after the War.

TAKING AIM

On this British fighter, the S.E.5a (S.E. meant 'scout experimental'), there are two types of gunsight – a ring-and-bead sight on the left used for close range, and an Aldis sight on the right, which contained lenses to see longer distances. There was a Vickers machine gun installed inside the nose, and on a special mounting above the upper wing was a drum-fed Lewis machine gun (above).

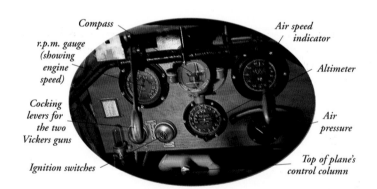

Compass

r.p.m. gauge (showing engine speed)

Cocking levers for the two Vickers guns

Ignition switches

Air speed indicator

Altimeter

Air pressure

Top of plane's control column

CAMEL COCKPIT

Most successful of all British fighters was the Sopwith Camel. It was said that looking ahead from a Camel cockpit was the most exciting view in the world, partly because the pilot looked over his two Vickers machine guns. By this time fighter cockpits had more instruments. The ignition switches were clumsy circular units with brass covers exactly like light switches in 1916 houses.

DOGFIGHT

By 1917 it was common for dozens of aircraft to engage in what became called 'a dogfight'. Each pilot tried to get on the tail of an enemy in order to shoot him down, whilst at the same time preventing any other enemy from getting on his own tail. Thus, he needed eyes in the back of his head. Here a Spad of RFC No. 23 Squadron tries to get on the tail of a Fokker D.VII marked with the simpler black cross which Germany introduced in 1918.

SPAD XIII

In 1915 French aircraft designer Louis Bechereau decided to use a completely new engine made by the Hispano-Suiza company (the name means 'Spanish-Swiss' and is better known as a car manufacturer). It had eight water-cooled cylinders in two rows and gave 150 horsepower. The result was an excellent fighter called Spad VII, and 5,600 were made. Next came the Spad XIII, with the engine uprated to 220 horsepower, armed with two Vickers guns. No fewer than 8,472 were made by 1918.

BRISTOL FIGHTER

Officially called the Bristol F.2B, this was unusual in that it was a successful fighter with a crew of two. In both World Wars, the way to shoot down an enemy was to get 'on his tail' and get the hostile aircraft in one's gunsight. While the Bristol pilot did this, the observer in the rear cockpit had either one or two Lewis machine guns which he could aim anywhere to the rear.

LEWIS MACHINE GUN

This gun was ideal for use by observers (backseaters), because it worked well even on its side or upside down, and was fed by a drum on top (holding either 47 or 97 rounds). Drums could be changed in seconds, the empty drum often being thrown overboard. The barrel was inside a fat casing containing cooling fins.

DEWOITINE D.520

In 1939 the French Dewoitine company began making the D.520, generally considered the best French fighter of the Second World War. Its 910-horsepower engine was made by Hispano-Suiza, and it was specially arranged so that a big 20mm cannon could fit on top of the crankcase firing through the hub of the propeller. The D.520 also had two machine guns in each wing, and had a top speed of 530 km/h (329 mph).

BOEING F4B-1

The F4B family were US Navy counterparts of the Hawker Fury. They had another kind of engine in which the cylinders were arranged radially like the spokes of a wheel and covered in thin fins so that they could be cooled by air. The resulting aircraft looked much less streamlined, but in fact the air-cooled radial was usually lighter. As it was also shorter it made the fighter more manoeuvrable, and it did not need a heavy drag-producing water radiator.

THE CHANGING ENGINE

In the First World War many fighters had rotary engines such as the 130-horsepower Clerget (left). The entire engine rotated together with the propeller, and this acted like a top (a gyroscope) and made piloting difficult. After 1918 designers made static radials, such as the 450-horsepower Bristol Jupiter (right). Apart from having nine instead of seven cylinders, this differed in using ordinary petrol (gasoline) without lubricating oil having to be added.

Between the World Wars

he First World War ended on 11 November 1918. For the next ten years there was little pressure to build better fighters, though engines developed dramatically. This development was further spurred by air racing. In 1931 a Rolls-Royce engine for racing developed 2,780 horsepower, though only for minutes at a time and using special fuels. Compared to the 130-horsepower engines on some fighters in the First World War, this was a huge leap and triggered the development of much better fuels for air force squadrons.

Also, by 1930, a few designers were finding out how to make aircraft with a metal skin. The wire-braced biplanes of the past had fabric covering and these were replaced by all-metal 'stressed-skin' monoplanes. This so dramatically reduced drag that fighter speeds jumped from 322 km/h (200 mph) to over 563 km/h (350 mph). In turn this led to cockpits covered by transparent canopies, improved engine installations, flaps on the wings to slow the landing, and landing gears that could retract in flight. Some of these developments were opposed by fighter pilots, who could not believe that a fighter could be a sleek monoplane with an enclosed cockpit.

POLIKARPOV I-153

This Soviet biplane was unusual among biplanes in having retractable landing gear. The wheels folded directly backwards, at the same time rotating through 90 degrees so that they could lie flat in the underside of the aircraft. The I-153 had a radial engine, but it was enclosed in a neat cowling to reduce drag. Thus, this fighter could reach 430 km/h (267 mph), about 100 km/h (62 mph) faster than the Fury and F4B.

HAWKER FURIES

In the days before jet aircraft there were two basic kinds of engine. Some had their cylinders (usually 12) cooled by water and arranged in two lines. When installed in the aircraft they resulted in a long and pointed nose, as in these Fury fighters of the Royal Air Force (RAF) in 1932. This looked very streamlined, but in fact to cool the water such engines needed a big radiator and this slowed the aircraft down.

FAMOUS FIGHTERS

Whereas the Allies in the Second World War used dozens of different fighters, the German Luftwaffe relied on 33,000 Bf 109s, later joined by 20,000 Fw 190s. The Messerschmitt Bf 109 (in the distance) was first flown in April 1935, but by fitting more powerful engines and heavier armament it was kept formidable to the end of the War. Some Bf 109 pilots managed to shoot down over 300 enemy aircraft. The Spitfire (in the foreground) was the most successful Allied fighter and also the most famous. A later and more advanced design than the Hurricane, the Spitfire was developed through 24 versions, starting in 1938 weighing 2,495 kg (5,500 lb) and a speed of 583 km/h (362 mph) and ending in 1945 weighing (5,269 kg (11,615 lb)) and with a speed almost 160 km/h (100 mph) greater!

HAWKER HURRICANE

Compared with the Bf 109 the British Hurricane was rather more primitive in design, being larger and, until 1941, covered in fabric like a fighter of the First World War. Major advantages of the Hurricane were that it was easy to fly, very tough and easy to repair. In the Battle of Britain, Hurricanes shot down more German aircraft than everything else combined.

AFTER THE BATTLE

By the end of the War towns and villages throughout Europe bore the scars of air attack. This town in Normandy (northern France) was actually fought over in 1944. Just outside would have been the RAF fighters, based on a hurriedly constructed airfield with the pilots living in tents. The runway would be a bulldozed field with a long strip of steel mesh laid down to give a smooth surface.

LEADERS OF THE LUFTWAFFE

In 1933 the German air force, forbidden after 1918, was reborn as The Luftwaffe. The Commander was Field Marshal Hermann Goering, who was to become a significant Nazi leader over the War period, and he appointed Ernst Udet (right) to choose the planes. Both men were fighter aces in the First World War.

The Second World War
The War in Europe

The Second World War (1939–45) firmly established the military role of aeroplanes. The Battle of Britain, which in the summer and autumn of 1940 certainly changed the entire course of history, was the first time since 1918 that large numbers of fighters had engaged in deadly air combat. This time, virtually all the fighters were streamlined stressed-skin monoplanes, with engines of over 1,000 horsepower and maximum speeds significantly higher than 480 km/h (300 mph). The combined Allied air forces in Britain were outnumbered by the German Luftwaffe (air force), and also had the disadvantage that Britain's airfields had been heavily bombed. However, the British had one huge advantage – the invention of radar. Instead of fighters flying aimlessly waiting for an enemy encounter, every Luftwaffe attack was plotted and pilots were given accurate directions for interception.

SPITFIRE PILOTS

The Second World War began in September 1939, and by the end of 1940 the RAF had lost more pilots than it had at the start. It was thus extremely important that hundreds of pilots found their way to England from the countries overrun by Germany, such as Poland, Czechoslovakia, France, Belgium, the Netherlands, Denmark and Norway. Many others came from Commonwealth countries such as Canada, Australia, South Africa and New Zealand. Without them Britain's situation would have been even more serious.

The Second World War
The War in the Pacific

PEARL HARBOR

The Imperial Navy used three main types in their carefully planned surprise attack: the 'Zero' fighter, the Aichi D3A dive bomber and the Nakajima B5N torpedo bomber. All were quite ordinary aircraft, but their combined attack proved devastating. For the US Navy there was only one bit of good fortune: their vital aircraft carriers were away at sea, and so survived. Later, it was to be the aircraft from those carriers that were to destroy the mighty Japanese fleet.

On 7 December 1941 the Japanese Imperial Navy Air Force attacked the US Pacific Fleet at Pearl Harbor, in Hawaii. This act brought both countries into the War. At that time almost nothing was known about Japanese aircraft, the Allies having the idea that they were all flimsy inferior copies of American and British designs. Nothing could have been further from the truth! One fighter alone, the Navy Mitsubishi A6M2, commonly known as the Zero, shot down with ease every Allied aircraft it encountered. This was surprising as it had an engine of only just over 1,000 horsepower. After this shock, Japanese aircraft were taken very seriously. By 1944 many Japanese were flying Kamikaze suicide missions, deliberately crashing their bomb-laden aircraft on to Allied ships. Fighters found it difficult to defend against such attacks. Towards the end of the War, the Japanese best was the Nakajima Ki-84 Hayate (Gale). Gradually such aircraft as the US Navy F6F and F4U gained the upper hand.

KAMIKAZE PILOTS

In the final year of the War thousands of Japanese chose to undertake many kinds of suicide mission. These pilots had volunteered for Kamikaze missions. The Kamikaze was a great wind which hundreds of years earlier had scattered an enemy fleet. In October 1944 Japanese pilots first decided to load up their aircraft with explosives and crash them on enemy ships in the Philippines, and later at Okinawa. By 1944 the Imperial Navy even had tiny rocket aircraft, so fast they were almost impossible to shoot down, with the whole nose filled with explosives.

ADVERSARIES
IN THE SKY

Apart from the Imperial Army's Kawasaki Ki-61, all the mass-produced Japanese fighters had air-cooled radial engines. By 1943 these engines had been developed to over 1,900 horsepower, and this made possible even more formidable fighters. By this time such US Navy fighters as the F6F Hellcat (right, taking off from an aircraft carrier) and F4U Corsair had achieved supremacy over the 'Zero' and other 1,000-horsepower types, but the Imperial Army's Nakajima Ki-84 (left) was typical of the new species. Though it did not quite reach 644 km/h (400 mph), the Ki-84 was a brilliant all-round aircraft. However, most of the Japanese pilots were inexperienced, and they never again got the upper hand.

A JAPANESE ZERO

The Zero only had just over 1,000 horsepower, but it was so light it could outfly its opponents, and then destroy them with its two 20mm cannon.

ENOLA GAY

In great secrecy the USA, assisted by British scientists, had invented atomic bombs, one of which could destroy a city. On 6 August this B-29, named 'Enola Gay' after the aircraft commander's wife, dropped such a bomb on Hiroshima. Three days later another, named 'Bock's Car', dropped a different kind of bomb on Nagasaki. The Japanese surrendered.

RECOGNITION BOOK

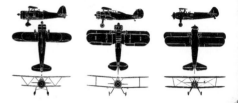

To the inexperienced eye, all aircraft (with some exceptions) look quite similar. Recognition manuals became standard issue for fighter pilots although many never became skilled at telling friend from foe. This page from a 1941 recognition book shows (from the left): a Fiat C.R.42, an Italian fighter; a Gloster Gladiator, a British fighter; and a Boeing (Stearman) PT-13, an American trainer.

THE SECOND WORLD WAR

This pilot (right) is wearing standard British flying clothing. The one-piece overall was pulled on from below and fastened with zips. In the front of the legs are pockets for maps and other documents (though pilots had to be very careful what they took with them over enemy territory). Most operational clothing could be plugged in and electrically heated. He is actually wearing his oxygen mask, so with goggles in place no part of his face is visible. His kit is completed by long cape-leather gloves and sheepskin-lined boots, and his seat-type parachute is on the ground.

PARATROOPS

This Italian magazine of about 1940 is making propaganda out of Italy's parachute troops, which used to descend from the sky to capture enemy targets. Such a means of attack was pioneered in the Soviet Union, and then adopted on a large scale by the Germans. Thousands of paratroops were used in Belgium in 1940 and to capture Crete in 1941. Even larger numbers were used by the British and Americans in 1944-5.

BETWEEN THE WARS

In the 1920s it gradually became universal for fighter pilots to wear parachutes. This Belgian pilot is wearing a British Irvin type of pilot parachute, with the canopy and shroud lines all tightly folded inside a pack which formed a cushion on which the pilot sat. The fighter's seat was an aluminium 'bucket' type with a big hollow in which the parachute fitted. He wears a leather helmet, goggles (because he had an open cockpit) and cavalry type boots.

Fighter Pilots of the Past

It seems astonishing today that the fighter pilots of the First World War did not have parachutes and were not even strapped in to their cockpits. One of the greatest British aces, Major Albert Ball VC, was found one day lying dead on the ground. There was no aircraft near, and no German claimed to have shot him down, and it was thought he must have simply fallen out of his fighter. By the mid-1930s the fighter pilot climbed into his cockpit, sat on his parachute, strapped tightly into his seat, and then had to plug in both his radio cable and oxygen pipe. Training programmes were also developed. Pilots would learn on simple primary trainers, and after as little as 40 hours, they would progress to more powerful trainers, such as the T-6 Texan (or Harvard). At something over 150 hours they would progress to operational fighters and would practise firing at targets towed on a long cable by special tug aircraft. By 1942 pilots were learning to drop bombs and fire rockets, both challenging tasks as the weapons had no inbuilt guidance as they do today.

MUSTANG PILOT

In the Second World War one of the best Allied fighters was the North American P-51 Mustang. This pilot would have much in common with pilots of the past, but much more equipment. His helmet would be fitted with headphones, and on the front it carried an oxygen mask (note the big pipe going to it) and integral microphone.

WASPS

In the USA there were so many women pilots that many of them were organized into the Women's Auxiliary Service Pilots to ferry all kinds of aircraft from factory to squadron, and often to repair or modification centres.

Night Fighters

BRISTOL BEAUFIGHTER

The Beaufighter was a massive, powerful and tough long-range fighter with devastating armament of four cannon and six machine guns. Once it was equipped with radar it proved ideal as a night fighter, entering RAF service in this role in late 1940.

A few aircraft in the First World War were intended for fighting at night, especially against airships, but the technology for such a task did not exist. By the Second World War it was commonplace for aircraft to fly at night, but it was still almost impossible to hunt down enemy aircraft on a dark night. The breakthrough was the development of radar sets small enough to be carried inside aircraft. Such AI (Airborne Interception) radar comprises boxes of electronics and various antennas. These aim an electronic beam into the sky ahead, while other antennas pick up reflections from enemy aircraft. Primitive AI in 194 was bulky and heavy, and needed skilled operators. Thus, the AI-equipped fighter had to be large and powerful. The first successful type was the Bristol Beaufighter, used in the War to shoot down Luftwaffe bombers, and later to fire torpedoes and rockets against enemy ships. In 1942 came the de Havilland Mosquito. Faster than the 'Beau', this brilliant aircraft served as a bomber, a day and night fighter and attack aircraft, a long-range reconnaissance aircraft and even for goods transport. Soon the Luftwaffe was fitting radars into their aircraft, and from 1943 they also added a new kind of armament installation, in the form of powerful cannon firing at a steep angle upwards. This meant they could attack from underneath and Allied planes literally never knew what hit them.

MOSQUITO COCKPIT

The de Havilland Mosquito was even better than the Beaufighter. Though it was made of wood, it was one of the fastest aircraft in the sky, and it could fly almost any kind of mission. The pilot sat on the left in a rather 'cosy' cockpit, with the navigator on his right, just far enough back for elbows not to clash. Here the pilot's controls of a Mk XII night fighter are on the left, beyond the top of his control column, with its gun-firing button. On the right are the radar displays and controls, managed by the navigator.

LUFTWAFFE NIGHT FIGHTER

First flown in May 1936, the Messerschmitt Bf 110 was planned as a formidable twin-engined, long-range fighter to escort the Luftwaffe bombers. In the Battle of Britain they proved easy targets for Hurricanes and Spitfires, but were about to become very useful. Fitted with more powerful DB 605 engines, and with a crew of three, they were packed with radar in order to find RAF bombers at night. This late-1944 Bf 110G-4B/U1 has a mass of radar antennas on the nose, as well as special exhausts which showed no visible flames at night.

THE BEST NIGHT FIGHTER PILOT

Major Heinz Wolfgang Schnaufer shot down an amazing 121 RAF heavy bombers at night. He survived the War, only to be killed soon afterwards in a traffic accident.

SCHRÄGE MUSIK

This is German for 'slanting music', or jazz. It was their code-name for a special kind of armament for night fighters. Two or more heavy cannon would be installed in the middle of the fighter, pointing steeply upwards at 70 to 80 degrees. Skilled pilots would find an RAF heavy bomber and, carefully formating underneath it, would aim the guns at the spars of the wing. A quick burst, and the bomber would lose a wing. Provided the fighter got out of the way of the falling bomber there was no danger, because the RAF bombers were totally 'blind' underneath.

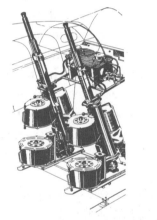

BLACK WIDOW

In the USA Northrop created one of the first aircraft ever planned as a night fighter from the outset. This big machine had a bulging central nacelle packed with radar, guns and a crew of three. The tail was carried on two booms. Fully loaded the P-61 Black Widow weighed up to 15 tons.

The First Jets

Towards the end of the Second World War, the engines of the latest war planes were cumbersome masses of metal weighing over a ton, yet with every part made like a fine Swiss watch. Even though the latest fighters had become heavier, the massive engines could propel them at over 724 km/h (450 mph). The difficulty was that it was almost impossible to make traditional fighters go any faster. Even more serious was the fact that ordinary propellers were reaching a fundamental speed limit. Thus the fighters of 1944-45 were the end of an era. In both Britain and Germany the turbojet engine was being developed. Frank Whittle had invented the first turbojet engine in Britain in 1929 but nobody was interested. Six years later in Germany, Hans von Ohain thought of the same idea, and the first jet aircraft flew in Germany in August 1939.

Nothing much happened to Whittle's engine until one was sent to the USA. Then things moved fast, and the first Allied jet fighter, the American Bell P-59 Airacomet, flew on 2 October 1942. However, the much greater German effort resulted in a shoal of jet aircraft. The most important was the Messerschmitt Me 262, and had the Germans not been defeated in 1945 their jets would have been a big problem for the Allies.

A NEW BREED OF PILOT

R.P. 'Bee' Beamont was a fighter pilot throughout the War, and afterwards he became even more famous in Britain as a test pilot. He tested Hawker Typhoons and Tempests, followed by Gloster Meteor jets and many other types, before becoming Chief Test Pilot on the Canberra jet bomber, Lightning, TSR.2, Jaguar and Tornado.

ROCKET INTERCEPTOR

The Messerschmitt Me 163B was a strange tailless rocket interceptor with the pilot in the nose along with two 30mm cannon. Behind him were tons of deadly liquids which fed a rocket engine in the tail. It was a tricky 'last-ditch' weapon which killed many of its own pilots,

GLOSTER METEOR

First of the British jets, the Gloster Meteor had two Whittle-type engines, and first flew in March 1943. This was one of the prototypes, as indicated by the big 'P' in a circle. After the War a later version set a speed record at over 975 km/h (616 mph).

MESSERSCHMITT Me 262A-1A

The Me 262 was a superb all-round fighter and fighter-bomber powered by two Jumo 004B turbojets slung under the wings. In the nose was the formidable armament of four 30mm cannon. With a speed of 845 km/h (525 mph), it was much faster than any Allied aircraft. The Me 262 would have been even more of a problem to the Allies had not Adolf Hitler misguidedly decreed that they all be used as bombers.

LAVOCHKIN La-7

At the end of the Second World War the Russians had no jet aircraft, and typical of their fighters was the La-7, powered by a 2,000-horsepower piston engine. For the desperately harsh conditions on the Russian front aircraft had to be very tough and simple. The La-7 was nevertheless at least equal to fighters from any other country.

SIR FRANK WHITTLE

As a young and very junior RAF pilot in 1929 Frank Whittle invented the turbojet. He proved mathematically that it could work, but his superiors in the Air Ministry were not interested. At his own expense he took out a patent, finally granted in January 1930, but still nobody showed the slightest interest. At last, in desperation, he and a group of friends found just enough money actually to build a turbojet, which he started up on 12 April 1937. This amazed the officials and experts, but by this time hundreds of engineers were working on jets in Germany, and theirs was the first jet aircraft to fly.

GIANT AIRCRAFT CARRIERS

After the Second World War the US Navy began building aircraft carriers much bigger than any previous warships. Today 13 are in service, each with a displacement of up to 102,000 tons. The flight deck is over 300 metres (1,000 ft) long, and there are over 40 mess decks (restaurants) for the 6,000 ship's crew and aircrew on board. Each evening those off duty have a choice of 25 cinemas. When in action the rapid launch and recovery of aircraft is almost like a ballet, with different coloured deck crews each playing a choreographed role.

LANDING ON A CARRIER

This Boeing F-18 Hornet is about to hit the deck of a US Navy carrier. The pilot has lowered the landing gear and the long arrester hook at the tail, and put the wing in the high-lift configuration with the leading and trailing edges all hinged sharply downwards. Guided by electronic systems (in the old days pilots were guided by a batsman standing on deck with things like brightly coloured table-tennis bats) the pilot aims to hit the deck just beyond the first of several arrester wires stretched across the ship. The long hook should pick up one of these strong cables even before the wheels slam brutally on to the deck. The momentum of the aircraft pulls the wire out, resisted by a system of cable drums, stopping the aircraft sharply.

THE SEA VIXEN

This big de Havilland aircraft had powerful radar in the nose operated by a second crew-member in what was called 'the coal hole' low down on the right of the pilot. The armament was a mixture of four large guided missiles and various rockets or bombs. Vixens could dive faster than sound.

Naval Jets

From the earliest days of fighters attempts had been made to operate them from warships. Naval planes had been launched from lighters (flat barges) towed behind fast destroyers. In the Second World War fighters operated from British, American and Japanese aircraft carriers. Most did not last long, because they tended to crash on returning to the ship.

But by the end of the War, in August 1945, aircraft designers knew how to make naval aircraft strong enough to stand up to the violent stresses of being shot off catapults, smashed down on heaving decks and then suddenly brought to a halt by arrester wires. There was also a need to have folding wings, so that they could be taken down in small lifts and tightly packed in hangars.

By the time peace returned jet fighters were taking over, with improved electronic navigation aids. In the 1950s a series of new ideas were introduced: the angled flight deck, the powerful steam catapult, and the mirror sight to help guide pilots on deck in bad weather.

UNFOLDING THE WINGS

This Grumman F9F of the US Navy's 'Blue Angels' aerobatic team is unfolding its wings before being catapulted off the deck of an aircraft carrier. Naval aircraft are designed to fold their wings so that more can be packed into congested hangars below deck. The F9F entered service soon after the Second World War, and saw service in the Korean War of 1950-3.

SIDEWINDER MISSILE

The Sidewinder was invented by the US Navy in 1953 as a guided missile able to home (steer itself) on to the heat radiated by a target aircraft. Originally weighing only just over 45 kg (100 lb), it was the simplest and cheapest guided missile in its class. The heat-seeking guidance was in the nose, steering the missile via the four pivoted nose fins. Next came the warheads, followed by the rocket motor. On the fixed tail fins were small flywheels which spun at high speed to give the weapon stability. They are named after a venomous snake which in the same way senses heat emitted by its victims.

Supersonic Fighters

LIGHTNING

The prototype of this outstanding British fighter first flew on 4 April 1957. On the same day the Government said fighters were obsolete and that the RAF did not need any! This crippled the development of the Lightning, and the RAF and British aircraft industry took years to recover. Uniquely, the Lightning had a wing swept back at 60 degrees and two Rolls-Royce Avon turbojets one above the other. The bulge underneath is an extra fuel tank, and the small projections on each side of the nose carried missiles (not fitted here). The Lightning could reach twice the speed of sound.

In 1945 documents captured from Germany showed that jets could be made to fly faster if their wings were 'swept' (angled back like an arrowhead). The first such fighter to fly (in 1948) was the North American F-86 Sabre. It was 161 km/h (100 mph) faster than 'straight-wing' jets and in a dive it could fly faster than sound. Residents of Los Angeles began hearing strange bangs, and it was soon realized that they were caused by the supersonic fighter's shockwaves reaching the ground. Designers began to fit more powerful engines so that fighters could fly faster than sound on the level. The Convair F-102, a radar-equipped interceptor with a delta (triangular) wing and fin, was supposed to be supersonic but proved too slow. In 1954 it was urgently redesigned according to new aerodynamic discoveries and it reached Mach 1.25 (1.25 times the speed of sound) with the original engine. By 1956 it was developed into the F-106, exceeding Mach 2 and setting a record at 2,454 km/h (1,525 mph). Many countries added to the sophistication of design, engine power, and aerodynamics of the supersonic fighter but no other aircraft yet has matched the Soviet MiG-31 and MiG-31M for their combined speed and range, their power, radar ability and enormous air-to-air missiles.

A DOUBLE DELTA

The Swedes called their Saab 35 Draken (Dragon) a double delta because it had a delta wing mounted on the ends of an inner wing of even more extreme delta shape. Thus, all the fuel tanks, electronics and other items were arranged from front to rear. Despite its amazing shape, the Draken prototype, flown in 1955, was very successful, and eventually Saab built 600 including a few for Denmark and Finland. Some were passed on from Sweden to the Austrian air force. Drakens had the same engine as the Lightning, but half as many.

DELTA-WING FIGHTER

The F-102A had wings and vertical tail that were in a perfectly triangular shape (named 'delta' after the Greek letter). This shape enables the wing to be very thin yet stronger than wings of ordinary shape, and the short span (distance from tip to tip) makes it suitable for supersonic speeds. The penalty of small wings is the need for longer runways as such aircraft need to take off and land at high speeds.

'MISSILE WITH A MAN IN IT'

This is what Lockheed called their F-104 Starfighter when it was revealed in 1956. It was designed to meet the criticisms of US pilots who had fought in the Korean War and had been outflown by the MiG-15. It was designed to climb very steeply and fly faster than any enemy plane. Features included a single powerful engine, tiny razor-edged wings, a high tailplane and a pilot seat that ejected downwards.

'CHUCK' YEAGER

Major (later General) Charles E. Yeager was a fighter pilot in the United States Army Air Force (USAAF) during the Second World War. In peacetime he became a test pilot and flew the Bell XS-1 to become the first human to fly faster than the speed of sound on 14 October 1947.

Today's Pilots

The enormous increase in military flying in the Second World War led to rapid technical advances of all kinds, though many did not come into use until the conflict was over. Several of these developments affected pilots' clothing. In a steep turn, with the wings banked to an angle of 60 degrees, the acceleration is 2g (twice gravity), so your weight appears to have doubled. Planes at the end of the Second World War could reach about 6g, so the pilot had to keep a tight hold of the stick (control column) to stop his arm being wrenched off downwards. A sustained 6g turn will make most people 'black out'; they remain conscious but their eyes go dark and they can no longer see. Vision is restored on recovery to straight and level flight. To help counter this and other problems of violent manoeuvres, a special kind of flying clothing was developed.

COMBAT SIMULATOR

Whereas flight simulators help pilots to learn to master their aircraft, a combat simulator trains him to dogfight with enemy aircraft. It is inside a giant dome, on the inside of which the pilot sees the ground, the sky and other aircraft. Today there are so many computer games that there are thousands of potential fighter pilots!

MODERN PILOT

Comfortable in a Mk 14 ejection seat, this fighter pilot is all kitted up ready for action. Modern fighter seats are very complex and cost

FIGHTER COCKPIT

This is the cockpit of an F-16 Fighting Falcon simulator. In the distance can be seen 'enemies'. The pilot gets all the information he needs from the large square displays in front of him, each like a clever reprogrammable TV. Some guide his flight and help him find enemies, while others tell him about his own aircraft. Whereas other fighters have a traditional big control column ('joystick'), the F-16 pilot flies holding a small grip shaped to fit his hand on the right edge of the cockpit.

BONEDOME HELMET

Today fighter pilots wear a strong but light helmet which protects their heads if they should be violently bumped against the cockpit canopy. In combat, pilots were sometimes knocked out when they wore floppy leather helmets.

BOOTS

Fighter pilots wear strong boots with long laces. These help him push hard on the rudder or wheel brake pedals and protect him if he has to eject.

Both the pilot's legs are encircled by strong straps, one above the knee and the other round the calf. On ejection, the legs are pulled in and the pilot's arms are also restrained to avoid hitting the cockpit or being injured by windblast.

'TOP GUN'

This Hollywood blockbuster starring Tom Cruise as a maverick US fighter pilot also stars two of today's top fighter planes – the Grumman F-14 Tomcat carrier-based fighter of the US Navy, and the Soviet MiG.

FIRING HANDLE

Between the pilot's thighs is the black and yellow striped firing handle. This triggers a complicated computer-controlled sequence on which his life depends.

THE FLYING SUIT

Even today the standard attire of a fighter pilot is the overall. This Japanese pilot is not ready to fly. His cap would be replaced by the complex 'bonedome' helmet with oxygen mask, communications and other services.

EJECTION!

After the Second World War it was found that jet aircraft could fly so fast that, in an emergency, the pilot could not just 'bale out'. To escape by parachute he had to be shot out. Gradually ejection seats were made safer (early types sometimes painfully damaged the spine) and today the Martin-Baker Mk 14 is typical of the refined types on offer. Modern seats are shot out by a propulsion system incorporating a rocket, which can be seen firing here. A small chute is deployed to slow the seat down. Finally the pilot is released from the seat as his own parachute deploys automatically.

Today's Fighters

It is remarkable that the history of the fighter plane has seen just 30 years of piston-engined fighters (1915-45) and over 50 years of jets. In this time fighters have become bigger and heavier, far more powerful, incredibly more complicated and much more expensive. An unexpected development in today's fighters is that instead of the fighter getting faster, it has almost gone in reverse. In 1954 the first supersonic fighters reached over Mach 1 and went on to reach Mach 2. The MiG-25 nudged Mach 3. At such a speed aircraft must travel in almost straight lines. To manoeuvre, that speed must be brought right down. The French Dassault Mirage family all reached Mach 2.2, but their latest fighter, the Rafale, cannot exceed Mach 1.8. Some of the greatest of today's fighters are products of the former Soviet design teams, such as MiG and Sukhoi. Both have twin engines hung under a very efficient wing which, merged into the body and with powerful horizontal tails and twin fins, gives it outstanding manoeuvrability.

THE GREATEST?

One of the largest modern fighters is the Sukhoi Su-27, designed in Moscow and produced by a factory in Komsomolsk-na-Amur in far Siberia. It could be clumsy and unimpressive, but in fact many experts consider it the most formidable in the sky. Powered by two AL-31 engines, it has tremendous performance, and such test pilots as Evgenii Frolov have demonstrated manoeuvres – such as the upward-tilt 'Cobra' – that no Western fighter can copy. Su-27s and various successors carry a spectrum of missiles far superior to anything currently available in the West.

A COBRA MANOEUVRE

This manoeuvre was first performed in 1989 by Sukhoi test pilot Viktor Pugachev. He astonished the world by rotating his aircraft, nose up, through 120 degrees and then back to horizontal, with the flight path remaining horizontal.

PRODUCTION LINE

In 1972 the USAF invited manufacturers to submit ideas for a 'light fighter', much cheaper than the massive F-15 Eagle then in production. There was no suggestion the winner would actually be put into production, far less adopted by the United States Air Force (USAF), but before long the General Dynamics F-16 Fighting Falcon had gained so many customers it had far surpassed the F-15. Today a product of Lockheed Martin, later versions of F-16 are still in production at this factory at Fort Worth, Texas.

COST OF MODERN FIGHTERS

In the Second World War a Spitfire cost about £6,000, but today a single F-22 (left) costs over £60 million. Thus, for the price of one modern fighter, one could in theory have bought 10,000 Spitfires.

FIGHTER ENGINE

Today all fighters have turbofan engines, in which the air coming in at the inlet is divided. Some is compressed and then goes through the combustion chamber and turbines, while the rest is bypassed and mixed with the hot gas at the back. This Russian AL-31FP is one of a pair fitted to the Su-27 (see page 28). It has a maximum thrust of 13,300 kg (29,320 lb), and a special feature is that its jet nozzle can be vectored (swivelled) to exert powerful control on the aircraft. On top are all the fuel controls, starter, electric generator, hydraulic pumps and other accessories.

SEA HARRIER

In the Falklands War in 1982 the British Aerospace Harrier of the RAF and Sea Harrier of the Royal Navy enabled the Argentine invaders to be defeated. Without these quite small aircraft it would have been impossible even to consider retaking the islands.
No other aircraft can rule the skies and also attack ground targets without needing an airfield. This is because of the development of jet nozzles which can be directed downwards so the aircraft can take off and land vertically.

RAFALE

France's next-generation fighter is the Rafale (French for 'squall'). Made by the Dassault company, which since 1955 has delivered thousands of Mirage fighters, the Rafale has two engines and a controllable foreplane just above and ahead of the delta wing. Different versions are being produced for the Armée de l'Air (air force) and Aéronavale (navy). This Rafale has a clumsy fixed probe on the nose for taking on fuel in flight; most flight-refuelling probes are retractable

A EUROFIGHTER COCKPIT

Best of the future European fighters is the Eurofighter, made by Britain, Germany, Italy and Spain in collaboration. Here, beyond the advanced ejection seat, can be seen the control column and then the instrument panel dominated by big multifunction displays. As far as possible these displays are blank, showing the pilot only what he needs to know. Should anything go wrong he can push buttons to find out as much detail as he wishes. In the centre of the windscreen is the optically flat glass of the computerized gunsight.

F-22 RAPTOR

This strange name, meaning a bird of prey, has been chosen for the most important fighter in production today, being produced by Lockheed Martin for tomorrow's USAF. It is a very large aircraft, yet because it is specially designed for what is called 'stealth' it will be almost invisible on enemy radars. It has a huge wing and large tailplanes, and all the missiles are carried internally. Beside the fuselage are the big lozenge (diamond) shaped air inlets for the jet engines.

Fighters for the Millennium

ntil the jet era new fighters could be designed, developed and put into production in a few weeks. Today, despite the availability of computers that can ash the time needed for complex calculations, the same sks can take anything up to 10 years. Thus, the Eurofighter as a detailed feasibility study in 1984, but will not enter rvice until after 2002. Co-operation between the four llaborating countries was slow but eventually the Euro-fighter flew in March 1994. However, when test flying began, it had long been obvious that future fighters should have vectoring nozzles, able to swivel so the plane could thrust in different directions. Such nozzles may be available at the Eurofighter's mid-life update in 2007. Shape is also central to the performance of future fighters – to reduce the size of the reflection on enemy radar screens. The Lockheed Martin F-22 Raptor, the newest fighter in the world, has two very powerful ngines whose nozzles can not only vector but also discharge the jets through lat slits. This is all part of the trend towards 'stealth' design, which makes them ardly detectable on enemy radar. After the F-22, the next generation is the JSF Joint Strike Fighter), a US multi-service programme in which Britain has a mall share. Some designs have powerful engines with the VTOL (vertical takeoff and landing) capability of the Harrier.

AIR SHOW

Around the world millions of people like to go to air shows. Some of these, such as Farnborough in England and Paris in France, are trade shows where new aircraft are demonstrated to possible customers. Others are purely for fun, where crowds are thrilled by formation aerobatic teams such as the RAF's Red Arrows (as shown here).

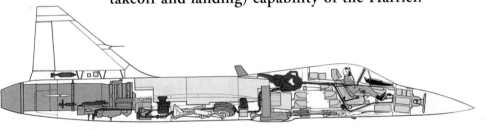

GRIPEN

Probably the smallest fighter in production in the world is Sweden's Saab Gripen (Griffin). It has an engine similar to that of the Hornet (see page 22) but one instead of two. Like the Rafale, the Gripen has a foreplane and a delta wing, a gun in the fuselage and missiles under the wing and on the wingtips.

DID YOU KNOW?

In the Soviet Union bombers were fitted with fighters to protect them. Vladimir Vakhmistrov conducted experiments that in November 1935 culminated in a TB-3 heavy bomber taking off with an I-15 biplane fighter on top of each wing and an I-16 monoplane fighter under each wing. An I-Z monoplane fighter then approached and hooked on under the fuselage, to make five fighters joined to one bomber! If enemy aircraft appeared they were all to unlatch and zoom off.

Arguments have raged over which was the first jet fighter. The first to fly was the German Heinkel He 280, which never went into production. The first to be delivered to a customer was the American Bell YP-59A Airacomet, delivered to the United States Army Air Force (USAAF) on 30 September 1943. The first delivered to a front-line regular squadron was the British Gloster Meteor, to 616 Squadron on 12 July 1944. And yet most experts think it should be the German Me 262. Suffice to say, in the Second World War, the Me 262 was the best jet fighter, and by far the most numerous.

The XF-85 Goblin unfolded its wings in flight. This tiny jet fighter had folding wings to fit inside one of the B-36 bomb bays. If enemy fighters appeared, the XF-85 was to be released. After dropping like a stone, its pilot would unfold the wings and do battle with the enemy. Afterwards he was to hook back on for the long ride home.

The fastest fighter in regular service was the Soviet Union's MiG-25. Powered by two huge R-15B-300 engines, it could fly long distances at 3,000 km/h (1,864 mph), or nearly three times the speed of sound.

In 1914 Pemberton-Billing designed, built and test-flew a successful fighter in seven days. The corresponding time for the development of the Eurofighter is 20 years (1982-2002).

In both World Wars a typical effective life for a fighter was two months. Today the RAF Jaguars are to serve 40 years (1972-2012), while the German Bachem Ba349 of 1944 was designed to fly a single mission only.

ACKNOWLEDGEMENTS

We would like to thank: Graham Rich, Del Holyland of Martin-Baker, Rosalind Beckman and Elizabeth Wiggans for their assistance.
Copyright © 2002 ticktock Entartainment Ltd.
First published in Great Britain in 1999 by ticktock Publishing Ltd., Century Place, Lambert's Road, Tunbridge Wells, Kent, TN2 3EH. All rights reserved.
No part of this publication may be reproduced, stored in a retrieval system, or transmitted in any form or by any means, electronic, mechanical, photocopying, recording or otherwise, without prior written permission of the copyright owner.
A CIP catalogue record for this book is available from the British Library. ISBN 1 86007 075 2

Picture research by Image Select. Printed in Egypt.

Picture Credits: t=top, b=bottom, c=centre, l=left, r=right, OFC=outside front cover, OBC=outside back cover, IFC=inside front cover

Ann Ronan@Image Select; 2tl, 2bl. AKG Photo London; OFC (dogfight) 7b, 12br, 12bl, 15tl. Aviation Photographs International; OFC (main pic: Francois Robineas, Dassault/Aviaplans, 3bl, 3br, 6tl, 7t, 8b, 9c, 11tr, 12tl, 15c, 18/19b, 20/21t, 21tr, 22tl, 22bl, 22/23c, 23tr, 24b, 25t & OFC, 26l, 28b, 30tl, 30/31c, 30cl. Bundesarchiv; 18/19c. Colorific; 31tr. FPG International; 14tl, 15b, 26tl, 30bl. Hulton Deutch; 13tr, 13b, 14b, 17bl, 21br. Hulton Getty; 4tl. Image Select; 3tl & OFC, 20bl. Kobal Collection; 27tr & OBC. Kozlowski Productions; 17tr & IFC. Mary Evans Picture Library; 3tr, 5tr, 5cr, 7cl, 7cr, 8/9t, 10t, 11br, 16c. Martin-Baker; 16/17c, OFC. Philip Jarrett; 6/7, 8tl, 10bl, 10br, 10/11c & OFC, 15tr, 18tl, 18bl, 19tr, 20/21b, 24tr, 29tr, 27bl, 29b & OBC. Quadrant Picture Library; 5b, 9t, 16tl & OFC, 20tl, 28tl, 26r. Salamander Picture Library; 4/5b & OBC, 9b, 12c, 16/17c & OBC+32, 23bl, 24/25c, 26bl, 31bl. Yefim Gordon; 29r,

Every effort has been made to trace the copyright holders and we apologize in advance for any unintentional omissions.
We would be pleased to insert the appropriate acknowledgement in any subsequent edition of this publication.

Journey

Alex Woolf

WS

HODDER
Wayland

an  Books

Produced for Hodder Wayland by
Discovery Books Ltd
Unit 3, 37 Watling Street, Leintwardine, Shropshire SY7 0LW, England

First published in 2003 by Hodder Wayland, an imprint of
Hodder Children's Books
This paperback edition published in 2004

© Copyright 2003 Hodder Wayland

British Library Cataloguing in Publication Data
Woolf, Alex
A Roman journey. - (History journeys)
1. Transportation - Great Britain - History - To 1500 - Juvenile literature 2. Great Britain - History - Roman period, 55B.C. -449 A.D. - Juvenile literature
I. Title
388' .09361'09015

0 7502 3949 2

Printed in China

Designer: Ian Winton
Editor: Rebecca Hunter
Illustrator: Mark Bergin

Hodder Children's Books would like to thank the following
for the loan of their material:

Ancient Art and Architecture: pages 9, 10 (top), 19 (middle), 27;
British Museum: pages 4, 5 (both); **Colchester Museum**: page 13 (bottom);
Corbis: *cover*, **Discovery Picture Library**: pages 12, 14, 15, 18, 19 (bottom), 21 (both), 25 (bottom); **Fortean Picture Library**: pages 23 & 25 (Janet & Colin Bord); **Museum of London**: pages 10 (bottom), 11 (Peter Froste); **Photo AKG London**: pages 6 (Peter Connolly), 7 (top Erich Lessing), 7 (bottom), 9, 16 (Erich Lessing), 17 (top Gilles Mermet), 17 (bottom Erich Lessing), 19 (top) & 20 (Erich Lessing), 24 & 26 (Peter Connolly), 27 & 29 (both) (Erich Lessing), 28 (Gilles Mermet); **Rebecca Hunter**: page 13 (top).

Hodder Children's Books
A division of Hodder Headline Limited
338 Euston Road
London NW1 3BH

CONTENTS

ROMANS IN BRITAIN

It is the year AD 208. Julius Gallicus is a Roman legionary who was born in Gaul (present-day France). He has been recruited by the Emperor Septimius Severus as part of the force to help stamp out an uprising by the Caledonian tribe in Britain at the northern border of the Roman Empire.

A Roman bust of the emperor Claudius. During his visit to Britain, Claudius accepted the surrender of eleven of the British tribal leaders.

Britain had been part of the Roman Empire for 165 years by the time of Julius Gallicus' arrival there. The invasion of Britain had taken place in AD 43. Claudius, the emperor at that time, sent a force numbering about 40,000 men under the command of Aulus Plautius.

BOUDICCA'S REBELLION

Boudicca was a queen of the Iceni tribe who led a rebellion in AD 60-1. After the Romans stole Iceni land and assaulted her and her daughters, she gathered a force of many thousands, and attacked and burned the Roman towns of Camulodunum (Colchester), Londinium (London) and Verulamium (St Albans). Her army was finally defeated by a Roman force under Suetonius Paulinus. Rather than being taken alive, Boudicca poisoned herself.

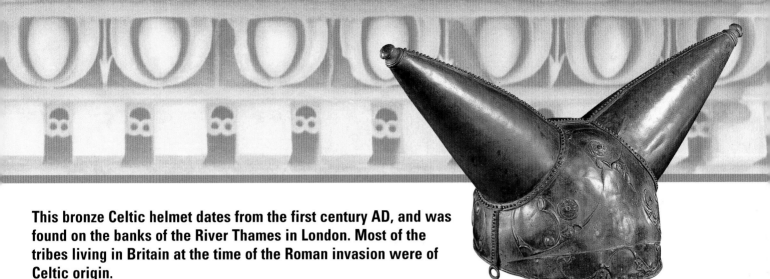

This bronze Celtic helmet dates from the first century AD, and was found on the banks of the River Thames in London. Most of the tribes living in Britain at the time of the Roman invasion were of Celtic origin.

At that time Britain was made up of many different tribes. There was no united response to the invasion, and the hastily gathered British army was no match for the highly trained legionaries. When news of the first victories reached Rome, Claudius himself came to Britain to witness the taking of Camulodunum (Colchester), which he declared should be the capital of the new Roman province. Within four years the invaders had conquered all of southern England and were making deep inroads into the north and west.

Britain remained part of the Roman Empire for the next 364 years. The Romans secured their conquest by building many towns and forts. These were connected by a network of roads to allow swift movement of troops and supplies. The towns were administered by tribal chieftains who had sworn loyalty to the emperor.

The Romans faced stern resistance to their rule in Scotland and eventually abandoned their plan of conquering the whole island. The emperor Hadrian ordered a wall to be built which marked the northern boundary of the empire.

The Celts protected themselves in battle with huge bronze shields almost the height of a man. These were often decorated with swirling patterns.

5

ROMAN SOLDIERS

Julius is 22 years old. He volunteered to join the army four years ago and he has yet to experience battle. He left his family in Lugdunum (Lyon) in present-day France knowing he might never see them again. Nevertheless he was excited at the thought of seeing the world, and attracted by the offer of a secure, well-paid profession.

A modern painting of a Roman legion on parade during the late first century AD. The ten cohorts are distinguished here by colour, each grouped into centuries. The legion also contains 120 horsemen.

Between 40,000 and 55,000 soldiers were stationed in Britain during the Roman occupation. They came from many different parts of the Empire, and by the time of Julius' arrival, many soldiers were being recruited from the local population in Britain.

The Roman army was organized into divisions of between 3,000 and 6,000 soldiers, called legions. The vast majority were foot soldiers, of which there were ten cohorts in each legion. The cohorts were further divided into centuries, each of 80 men, and these were led by centurions. Most recruits to the legions were between 18 and 22 years of age.

They would sign up for twenty-five years of service. By the second century AD, rebellions were rare in Roman Britain, and most soldiers would have spent little time actually fighting. They would be kept occupied with drills, training, route marches, and fort-building exercises.

This stone relief shows two Roman legionaries. One carries a gladius, or short sword, and shield, while the other carries a pilum, or spear.

The Roman army was highly disciplined, and punishments were severe. Theft or desertion were punishable by being beaten to death by comrades. Cowardice in battle could lead to decimation, which meant the execution of every tenth man in the guilty unit. The survivors were put on a ration of barley. Those soldiers who lived to retirement would receive some land and a regular income. Many soldiers in Britain remained in the province that had been their home for 25 years, and married local women.

This bronze Roman helmet dates from the early second century AD, and was discovered in Jerusalem in Israel. It is an 'Imperial Gallic' style of helmet, which had a large neck guard at the back.

CROSSING THE SEA

Julius and his fellow legionaries board the troop ship at the port of Gesoriacum (Boulogne). It is a slender, oak-built rowing ship with a team of twenty oarsmen. This is Julius' first time at sea. The crossing is rough, and he feels sick. He prays to Mercury, the god of travellers, that they will be delivered safely to Britain.

The main function of the Roman classis or fleet was to support the operations of the army. The Channel and the North Sea, with their strong tides and frequent storms, made life very difficult for Roman sailors, more used to navigating the almost tideless Mediterranean.

Some of the towns and roads in Roman Britain. Julius' journey is marked.

Nevertheless, the Roman fleet played an important part in the conquest and occupation of Britain by keeping the army well-supplied with equipment and reinforcements. In AD 83 the fleet helped in the attempted conquest of Scotland by making raids on the Scottish east coast. Some of these ships actually managed to circumnavigate Scotland, reaching the Orkney Islands, and proving that Britain was an island.

THE QUINQUEREME

The most successful warship of Roman times was a long slender ship called the quinquereme. It had three levels of oars, the top two being worked by two men, and the bottom by one. A common method of attack was to ram opposing ships with its heavy bronze beak fitted below the waterline, which could punch a hole in an enemy ship's hull.

This relief containing Roman galleys is part of Trajan's Column in Rome, which dates from the first century AD. The design of Roman warships was greatly influenced by the Greeks and the Phoenicians.

Most seaborne traffic, however, went to the port of London. In Roman times the Thames was beyond the reach of the tides, making it very easy to navigate. As well as London, Roman ports were also built at Dover and Richborough for ships crossing to or from Boulogne. There were also harbours at the Tyne, the Wash, Southampton and Exeter.

The Roman navy used oared warships and transport vessels, and sailing ships. Each ship was commanded by a trierarch and a centurion, and was manned by a small force of infantry, as well as rowers.

ARRIVING IN LONDINIUM

Julius is impressed by the port of Londinium, with over half a mile of waterfront crowded with barges and ships, their cargoes being unloaded. The quayside is thronged with soldiers, sailors and merchants. The legionaries disembark. They march to the fort where they will be lodging for the night. Outside they see slaves at work building the city wall.

(*Below*) Here is a model of a London waterfront scene in about AD 100. A cargo of amphorae (clay jars) is being unloaded from a ship, to be stored in one of the warehouses that line the quay.

The city of London was a Roman creation. There was a small Celtic settlement there before they arrived, but it was the Romans who saw the benefits of locating a city at the first point where the Thames could be bridged.

The new city grew quickly and was already a centre of trade when it was burned to the ground by Boudicca's army in AD 60. London was soon rebuilt, and replaced Colchester as the capital of the province. By the end of the first century AD, London had become established as Britain's commercial and political centre.

This modern painting shows an aerial view of how Londinium might have looked around AD 250. The town hall and market square are clearly visible in the centre of the city, and the army fort can be seen in the northwest, near the amphitheatre.

Fine public buildings were constructed to suit its status as an important Roman city, including temples, public baths and government buildings. The governor's palace was built beside the Thames, with large halls and a 35-metre garden pond with a fountain. The largest building in the city was the town hall. Next to it lay an impressive 3 hectare market square.

- 'London' is a Celtic word - perhaps deriving from the name of a farm or tribal chief from that area.

- The population of Roman London was between 12,000 and 20,000.

- In Roman times, the Thames was 300 metres wide (today it is 100 metres wide).

The fort where Julius and his fellow legionaries lodged was built around AD 120. It was situated on the northwest edge of the city, and housed the governor's guard. It was 200 metres square with rounded corner towers and a gate in each side. When Julius arrived in AD 208, a six-metre-high defensive wall was being constructed around the city, which included part of the wall around the fort.

A VISIT TO THE AMPHITHEATRE

The legionaries are off-duty for the remainder of the day. Julius and a few others decide to go and watch the games at the nearby amphitheatre. The climax of the show is a combat to the death between two helmeted gladiators. They are Samnites, who fight with oblong shields and short swords. Julius is pleased because his favourite wins.

The Roman theatre in Verulamium was built around AD 130, and was rediscovered in 1847. It is one of the few Roman theatres found in Britain.

Theatres and amphitheatres were built all over the Roman Empire, and remains have been found in Britain in places like Dorchester, Chichester and St Albans, as well as London. The amphitheatre in Londinium was initially a wooden structure, built in AD 70 at the northwest edge of the city just south of the fort. In AD 170 it was rebuilt in stone.

This fragment from a Roman relief shows another popular entertainment: gladiators were sometimes sent into the arena to fight wild animals such as lions and bears.

The games performed in these arenas were the most popular form of public entertainment in Roman times. The show would open with displays by troupes of acrobats. Entertainments also included animal baiting and wild beast hunts. Typical animals used in British amphitheatres were stags, wild boars, bulls and wolves.

The climax of the show was always a fight to the death between two gladiators. 'Gladiator' means 'swordsman', from the Latin gladius, 'sword'. They were usually slaves, prisoners of war, or criminals. Occasionally, female gladiators fought in the arena. There were various classes of gladiator: as well as Samnites there were Thraces who were armed with a small round shield and a curved dagger; they were generally pitted against mirmillones who had a helmet, sword and shield.

If a gladiator found himself at the mercy of his opponent, he lifted his finger to beg for salvation from the crowd. If the spectators wished him spared, they waved their handkerchiefs. But if they desired him to be killed they turned their thumbs downward.

A gladiatorial contest is shown on this Roman pottery vase found in Colchester. Here a defeated *retiarius* (right), in combat with a secutor, raises his finger for mercy.

13

ROMAN ROADS

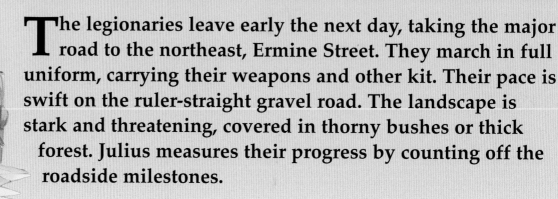

The legionaries leave early the next day, taking the major road to the northeast, Ermine Street. They march in full uniform, carrying their weapons and other kit. Their pace is swift on the ruler-straight gravel road. The landscape is stark and threatening, covered in thorny bushes or thick forest. Julius measures their progress by counting off the roadside milestones.

The Romans were remarkable road-builders. Archaeologists have traced more than 9,600 km of major Roman roads in Britain, as well as many more miles of minor roads and paths.

The roads were originally built to carry the soldiers and military supplies that enabled the conquest of Britain. They gradually came to be shared by other traffic – merchants, traders, couriers and government officials. Roads were the lifelines that kept remote garrisons supplied with food and materials, and allowed messages to be swiftly sent. A body of soldiers could cover up to 48 kilometres a day on these roads, carrying kit weighing 23 kilograms.

Blackstone Edge Roman road runs over the Pennines between Rochdale and Elland in South Yorkshire. Paved Roman roads like this one were quite unusual; most were surfaced with gravel or small stones.

Roman road-building techniques were similar throughout the Empire. An agger, or embankment, was built using the earth and stones dug up from either side, leaving ditches for drainage. Chalk or limestone provided a solid base on which gravel, broken flints or smaller stones were laid. When first built, Roman roads in Britain were about six metres wide. By AD 120 the width of most main roads averaged thirteen metres.

The Romans built their roads extremely straight. One stretch of the Roman-built Fosse Way never deviates more than 9.5 km from a straight line over its 320-km length. Military engineers achieved this by standing on high ground, and plotting each length of road in turn.

Repair and resurfacing of the roads was the responsibility of the civitates, or local authorities, based in the major towns of the province. They were also responsible for setting up milestones along the main roads, so that travellers could see the distance to the nearest town. Almost a hundred of these survive with their carved inscriptions still readable.

A Roman milestone at Chesterholm in Northumberland. Milestones were erected at every Roman mile (1,480m) along major roads. They were usually cylindrical in shape, up to 1.8 metres high and 45 cm in diameter. Inscribed on them was a mileage figure and the name of the town from which it was measured.

STAYING AT AN INN – Durovigutum

After two days, the legionaries reach Durovigutum (Godmanchester) which has a large mansio or inn. Here the weary soldiers wash off the sweat of the day's march in the bath-house before enjoying a good dinner. Most of the legionaries pass the final part of the evening in the tavern, but Julius prefers to go for a quiet stroll around the garden.

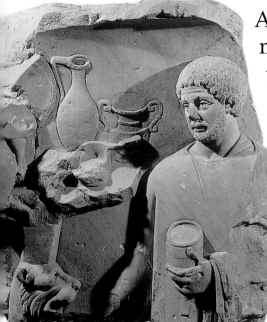

As the traffic increased on Roman roads, so mansiones were established to cater for travellers. They were spaced at 30- to 50-kilometre intervals, and provided meeting places for merchants and traders, rooms and refreshment for foot soldiers, and stables for messengers on horseback.

All mansiones followed a similar design, with the accommodation grouped around a central courtyard or garden. Many had separate bath-houses and exercise halls.

THE IMPERIAL MESSENGER SERVICE

In the first century BC, the Romans established the *Cursus Publicus*, or imperial communications service. A network of post-houses and mansiones were set up along the major roads throughout the Empire, including Britain. Couriers could get fresh horses at post-houses, set 15 to 25 kilometres apart, enabling them to cover about 80 kilometres a day.

This Tunisian mosaic shows dice players in a tavern. Gambling was a common activity in the taverns of Roman inns. A pair of dice were shaken in a cup and tossed. Bets were placed on the number they showed.

The mansio at Godmanchester was, by AD 208, one of the largest and finest in the country. The reception and dining rooms both had mosaic floors and plastered, painted walls. The bedrooms were arranged in two rows down the long sides of the building, and there may have been an upper floor of bedrooms as well.

There was a bath-house to the rear of the inn with separate changing rooms for men and women. Guests at the mansio could also make use of a number of shops and smithies (for horseshoes), and a small temple dedicated to the native god Abandinus.

These dice, which the Romans called tesserae, were made out of bone.

Sometimes mansiones led to the development of towns. The siting of a mansio at Chelmsford in the late first century AD was followed by the building of some shops, including a bakery, a dye-works, and some taverns. Before long, a small town had appeared.

THE BATH-HOUSE – Ratae Coritanorum

The Great Bath of Aquae Sulis (now Bath in Avon). This lay at the centre of an elaborate complex of five baths, built by the Romans above natural hot springs. Aquae Sulis also contained a great temple dedicated to the Celtic goddess, Sulis.

Two days later, the soldiers arrive at Ratae Coritanorum (Leicester), well-known for its fine public baths. The soldiers are keen to try them. Their shouts and splashes echo noisily around the stone chambers. Julius finishes with a massage and a dip in the cold plunge. Afterwards, he and his friends play a game of dice in the exercise yard.

The public bath was a very important part of Roman social life. It was the place for business deals, gambling, exercise and gossip. Visitors left their clothes in niches or cupboards in the undressing room, or they paid someone to look after them. From here they entered the frigidarium (cold room) where bathers could sprinkle themselves with water from a basin, or the bolder ones could jump into a large cold bath.

The Roman philosopher, Seneca, who lived above a public baths in the first century AD, was disturbed by 'shouts, grunts, slaps – and the screams of those who were having their armpits plucked.'

A bather's strigil. Once he had begun to sweat, the bather would pour olive oil on his body. Then the oil, along with any sweat and dirt on the skin, was scraped off with the curved metal blade of the strigil.

A first century AD case containing make-up tools. Roman baths contained women's dressing rooms, where women could spend time applying cosmetics and grooming themselves.

Bathers then moved into the tepidarium (warm room) where they oiled their bodies and felt the steam open their pores. They then had a choice of hot rooms – the caldarium with its dense steam, or the laconium, a dry-heat chamber. After a hot-water bath, the bathers reversed the route, ending with a dip in the cold pool to close the pores. The discovery of tweezers, earpicks and nail-cleaners at some bath-houses suggests that people could obtain other treatments too.

The baths were open all day. Women used them in the morning, and men in the afternoon and evening. They were heated by an under-floor central-heating system called a hypocaust. The public baths in towns like Leicester, Chichester and Wroxeter may have been used by up to 500 people a day.

This is the furnace used for heating the water at the large public bath-house at the Roman town of Viroconium (now Wroxeter in Shropshire).

GODS AND GODDESSES

As the legionaries progress northwards, the locals seem more hostile. Sometimes they spit at the soldiers. Julius is nearly hit by a stone. At Eboracum, Julius' fears are eased by the sight of the many statues to Roman gods and goddesses. At the temple of Mars he prays for the war god's help in the coming battles against the barbarians.

Jupiter, depicted in this second century AD statue, was the king of the Roman gods. Originally the god of the sky, Jupiter was worshipped as god of rain, thunder and lightning.

The Romans worshipped many different gods, each of which was associated with a different activity. The most important gods were Jupiter, Juno and Minerva. Jupiter was the most powerful god, who could be called upon to protect both the individual and the state. Juno was the goddess of women and childbirth, and Minerva the goddess of healing. Beneath them were gods such as Mercury who protected travellers and merchants, Apollo the god of music and healing, and Venus the goddess of love.

The Romans were usually tolerant of the religious beliefs of conquered peoples. They accepted and even worshipped some of the local Celtic gods, seeing similarities between them and their own gods. For example, the Romans associated the Celtic god Sulis with Minerva. Throughout Britain, temples and shrines were built to Celtic gods and their Roman equivalents.

Remains of a third century AD temple to Mithras at Carrawburgh on Hadrian's Wall. The worshippers of Mithras were divided into seven grades. To enter a new grade involved passing severe tests such as ordeals of heat, cold and fasting. An 'ordeal pit' has been found at Carrawburgh close to a large fire.

The temple priests wore robes and bronze or silver jewelled headbands. Worshippers brought offerings such as small figurines, jewellery, or a live sheep, which they laid before the altar. Some brought curse tablets, rolled-up sheets of lead on which they had scratched a plea to the god to punish a person who had wronged them.

A religious cult that gained particular popularity with the Roman army throughout the Empire during the second and third century AD was Mithraism. Mithras was the Persian god of light and truth. He encouraged physical and moral strength in his followers, increasing his appeal to soldiers. Five Mithraic temples have been found in Britain, including a famous one in London.

Three altars found at the temple at Carrawburgh. Each of these contain dedications to Mithras from soldiers who served at the fort.

REACHING HADRIAN'S WALL

The legionaries finally reach their destination: Hadrian's Wall – the edge of the Roman Empire. They have been travelling for twelve days, covering 463 kilometres. Julius climbs some steps to the top of the Wall. It winds over hills and valleys, disappearing over the horizon in either direction. He looks out across the barren empty lands beyond. There is no sign of the Caledonians.

Today, Hadrian's Wall is officially recognized as a World Heritage Site. The best-preserved sections of the Wall are about one metre high.

Hadrian's Wall was built on the orders of the emperor Hadrian following his visit to Britain in AD 122. He saw the need for a physical border between Roman Britain and the independent tribes to the north, to control the movement of people and goods, and to help defend the province from attack.

However, the Wall's main purpose was political, not military. It marked the northern limits of the Roman Empire, and was intended as a permanent line separating the barbarians to the north from the civilized world of the Romans.

The Wall runs from coast to coast for 117 kilometres between Wallsend-on-Tyne in the east, and Bowness-on-Solway in the west. It took 14 years to build and by AD 136 it was complete. However, it continued to be modified and improved over the years. In its final form it was a stone wall 4.25 to 4.65 metres high and 2.4 to 3 metres thick. On its north side was a ditch to make it more difficult to attack. To the south of the Wall was the Vallum, a flat-bottomed ditch with earthen mounds to either side. This was built to prevent civilians from gaining access to the Wall. Soldiers could reach the Wall via guarded causeways across the Vallum.

The Wall fell into neglect and disrepair during certain periods of the Roman occupation. When the Romans left Britain in AD 407, Hadrian's Wall no longer had a purpose. In the years that followed, many of its stones were taken away and used in the construction of local buildings.

The north gate of Vercovicium Roman Fort on Hadrian's Wall. The fort was one of twelve situated along the Wall. Vercovicium means 'the Place of Fighters'.

MANNING THE FORT

Julius is separated from his travelling companions, and sent to Vercovicium, one of the forts on the Wall. The following morning he reports to the praetorium, the largest building in the fort, where the commander lives with his family. After receiving a personal greeting from the commander, Julius joins the other legionaries and auxiliary soldiers of the fort in the assembly hall, where the orders of the day are read out.

A reconstruction of Vercovicium Fort showing how it might have looked in the third century AD. The vicus (civilian settlement) can be seen to the right of the fort, with the principias (headquarters) and praetorium (commander's house) in the centre.

All the way along Hadrian's Wall, small forts, called milecastles, were built at intervals of a Roman mile (1,480 metres). Each milecastle could house units of up to thirty men. There were seventeen milecastles in all, each containing between five hundred and a thousand troops. Between each milecastle were two evenly spaced towers where sentries kept watch. The plan was that every part of the Wall would be visible during daylight.

Larger forts were built at strategic points, which had barracks to accommodate up to 1,000 troops each. When the Wall was threatened, troops would pour out of the north gates of the forts and milecastles to confront the attackers.

The granaries at Vercovicium had vents in the outer walls and floors raised on stone pillars, to allow air to circulate. It was originally a single building, but was split into two in the third century AD.

Vercovicium contained thirteen barrack blocks, where the soldiers lived and slept. Each block was capable of holding a century (80 men). Food was stored in granaries, which had floors suspended on stone pillars to keep the food cool and dry and free of vermin.

Most forts had wells. However, Vercovicium obtained its water supply by collecting rainwater in tanks via a system of channels and drains. These tanks were also used to flush out the lavatories.

The lavatories at Vercovicium. Wooden seats would have been fitted in a row on each side directly over the main sewer. The two water channels in the centre would have been used by soldiers to wash the sponges that served the purpose of toilet paper.

HOSPITALS

Soldiers in the Roman army were more likely to die from disease than from battle wounds. The Romans were well aware of this risk and troops based at Hadrian's Wall were provided with a good standard of medical care. The hospital at Vercovicium contained a surgery, small rooms for staff and patients, and a courtyard for growing medicinal herbs.

MARCHING INTO BATTLE

The soldiers are patrolling the Wall north of Vercovicium. The Caledonians emerge waving spears and charging. Julius is scared, but remembers his training. The legionaries let fly with their javelins, striking the shields of the attackers. Before the enemy can recover, the Romans are upon them, forcing them back with their iron shield bosses and stabbing them with their short swords.

Legionaries were equipped with four weapons. The javelin was a kind of spear, over two metres in length, with a long, slender iron head on a wooden shaft. It could kill a person at a distance of 30 metres. High on his right side, the legionary wore a bronze gladius (short sword) which had a 50-centimetre, sharp-pointed blade. On his left, he carried an iron dagger. To defend himself, the legionary possessed a curved, rectangular shield made of leather-covered wood, bound with bronze strips and with an iron boss in the centre. His shield was useful as a weapon to push and batter the enemy.

Pieces of Roman armour found at the Roman fort at Corbridge, Northumberland. These form parts of a soldier's cuirass, or body armour, such as shoulder plates (1), breast plates (2) and girth hoops (3). In the centre are reconstructions of the pieces of a cuirass.

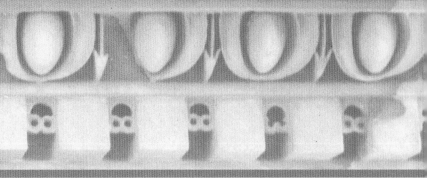

A stone relief from the early second century AD showing a barbarian fighting a Roman legionary. When fighting the Celts, Roman tactics involved getting in very close to the enemy for hand-to-hand fighting. The gladius proved more useful in these situations than the long Celtic sword.

In battle, the legionaries usually stood in the centre and provided the main thrust of the attack, with the cavalry positioned at the sides. Auxiliary units (support troops) fought on the wings or were held in reserve. Legionaries were trained to fight in a strict pattern of disciplined formations.

To overcome Celtic strongholds such as Maiden Castle or Hod Hill, the Romans used ballistas (missile launchers) to provide a continuous barrage of iron bolts. The attack might then be led by a testudo, or 'tortoise', a formation of 27 men arranged in four ranks who locked their shields overhead and on all sides to give all round protection.

BALLISTAS

These siege weapons resembled sophisticated crossbows, and were used against British hill-forts. They fired iron bolts, or sometimes stone balls, with great accuracy, and could kill at up to 365 metres. About fifty ballistas would be used during a siege.

MEALS AND LETTER HOME

Exhausted after the fight, Julius returns to the fort at Vercovicium, grateful to have survived his first battle. He shares a meal of bread, vegetable soup, mutton and wine with his comrades. Before going to sleep, Julius writes a letter to his parents back in Lugdunum, telling them of all his experiences.

A letter found at Chesterholm contained the following: 'I have sent you ..... pairs of socks from Sattua, two pairs of sandals and two pairs of underpants...'

(TAB. VINDOL. II.346)

A third century Roman mosaic from Tunisia showing the ingredients of a banquet: baskets of fruit and vegetables surrounding a gazelle. Rich Romans enjoyed dining on unusual or exotic foods, such as sow's udder, flamingo, and molluscs 'harvested under a waxing moon'.

A legionary paid for his food himself, costing him about a third of his year's wages. His basic ration consisted of wheat – which he could grind into flour – soup, vegetables, lard (pork fat), and meat. The usual drink was sour wine or vinegar. The choice of vegetables included beans, cabbage, celery and lentils, and the meat might be pork, beef, lamb, veal or goat.

Records found at Chesterholm and Vindolanda, show that supplies of exotic foods such as venison, spices and garlic were sometimes received for the garrison commander rather than the troops. However, occasional treats such as plums, olives and Spanish wine managed to find their way into the milecastles and watchtowers on Hadrian's Wall, judging from inscriptions on amphorae (clay jars) found there.

A second or third century stone relief of Romans eating dinner. Cena (dinner) was the main meal of the day, and consisted of at least three courses.

Like many forts on the Wall, Vercovicium had a small civilian settlement, or vicus, attached to it with taverns and shops. The soldiers could go there in their off-duty hours and purchase food to supplement their rations.

Tablets at Vindolanda reveal the prices soldiers had to pay for certain goods. For example, a towel cost 2 denarii and a cloak cost 5 denarii (legionaries earned about 300 denarii a year). To avoid these extra expenses, some soldiers wrote letters to their families asking for money or clothing or for a kind of food they missed.

The Roman army in Britain was gradually weakened from the middle of the third century AD. Troops were withdrawn to fight on other frontiers of the Empire. Meanwhile, Britain's coasts were increasingly threatened by Scots, Picts, Saxons and Franks. The rich moved to the comparative safety of towns, and villas were abandoned. The last soldiers of the Roman army finally left Britain in AD 407.

A stone relief showing a scene in a Roman bakery. Bread was the basis of the Roman soldier's diet.

29

TIMELINE

55/54 BC — Julius Caesar invades, but does not conquer Britain.

Late 1st century BC — *Cursus Publicus* – the Roman postal service established.

AD 43 — Romans under Claudius invade Britain and establish first Roman-British city at Colchester. Eleven British kings surrender to Claudius.

c. AD 43-45 — Watling Street is built.

c. AD 45-47 — Fosse Way is built.

c. AD 50s — Ermine Street is built.

AD 60/61 — Boudicca leads a rebellion against the Romans.

AD 75-77 — The conquest of Britain is completed.

AD 79 — Agricola, the provincial governor, invades Scotland.

AD 75-100 — London transformed into a Roman city.

Early 2nd century AD — London recognized as the provincial capital.

c. AD 120 — Godmanchester mansio and bath-house built.

c. AD 122 — Hadrian approved building of a chain of canals as supply routes between the Fens and York.

AD 122-136 — Hadrian's Wall is built.

c. AD 150 — Baths at Leicester built.

Late 2nd century AD — Development of York. Many public buildings and monuments erected, including Temple of Mars.

AD 197 — Caledonians break through the Wall and devastate northern England.

AD 208 — The emperor Septimius Severus comes to Britain with a large army to deal with the Caledonian uprising, and repair damage to the Wall. London city wall is built.

AD 209 — Caledonians surrender.

c. AD 240 — Temple of Mithras is built in London.

AD 350-400 — The Romans begin to leave Britain, as they struggle to defend their Empire closer to Rome.

AD 407 — The last Romans leave Britain.

GLOSSARY

amphitheatre — An oval arena surrounded by rising tiers of seats. These were used for many forms of entertainment.

amphora — A jar, usually made of clay, with a narrow neck and two handles, used by the ancient Greeks and Romans for holding oil, wine or certain foods.

auxiliary units — The second line of the Roman army, made up of soldiers who were not Roman citizens. They signed on for twenty-five years, and their reward on retirement was a grant of citizenship.

boss — A round raised area that sticks out of a surface, for example a stud at the centre of a shield.

Caledonians — Inhabitants of the northern part of Scotland during the Roman occupation of Britain. They were described by the Roman historian Tacitus as being 'red-haired and large of limb'.

Catuvellaunian — A member of the Catuvellauni - a tribe descended from the Belgae of northern France, and inhabiting the area of present-day Hertfordshire. The Catuvellauni were the dominant tribe in the southeast of Britain at the time of the Roman invasion.

causeway — A raised path over a ditch or area of water.

cavalry — The part of an army made up of soldiers trained to fight on horseback.

centurion — In ancient Rome, an officer in charge of a unit of 80 foot soldiers.

circumnavigate — Sail around something, such as an island.

civitates — A town council.

cohort — An ancient Roman military unit that formed one tenth of a legion and consisted of 300 to 600 men.

denarii — Plural of 'denarius' - an ancient Roman silver coin originally worth ten asses. A gold denarius was worth 25 silver denarii.

figurine — A small ornamental figure, often pottery or metal.

Fosse Way — A major Roman road which runs diagonally across Britain from Topsham in Devon to Leicester and Lincoln, probably built to serve a line of frontier forts in the early years of the conquest.

garrison — A body of troops stationed at a military post, or a military post where troops are stationed.

hypocaust — A furnace, fired by charcoal, wood or coal, that pumped hot air through channels beneath the floor of a room. Both heat and gases escaped through flues behind the walls, creating an early central-heating system.

legionary — A member of a Roman legion.

post-houses — Places established on the major roads of the Roman Empire where messengers of the imperial communications service could get a change of horse.

quayside — A platform that runs along the edge of a port or harbour, where boats are loaded and unloaded.

shrine — A place of worship.

smithies — Plural of 'smithy' - the place where a blacksmith works.

theatre — Theatres had a stage at one end surrounded by seats. They were used for plays and singing entertainments.

trierarch — A ship's captain in the Roman navy. He shared command of his vessel with a centurion, who was in charge of military aspects.

venison — The meat of a deer.

FURTHER READING

What Happened Here? Roman Palace, Tim Wood, A&C Black, 2000.

A Day in the Life of a Roman Centurion, Richard Wood, Hodder Wayland, 2000.

Pinpoints: The Living Roman Fort, Stephen Johnson, Hodder Wayland, 2001.

You Wouldn't Want to be a Roman Gladiator, John Malam, Hodder Wayland, 2001.

INDEX